FORTUNE'S FAVOR
SCOTT IN ANTARCTICA

ALSO BY KIM ROBERTS

POETRY

Fortune's Favor: Scott in the Antarctic
Animal Magnetism
The Kimnama
The Wishbone Galaxy

PROSE

Lip Smack: A History of Spoken Word Poetry in DC

EDITOR

Full Moon on K Street: Poems About Washington, DC

FORTUNE'S FAVOR

SCOTT IN ANTARCTICA

Kim Roberts

Poems by Kim Roberts

For Jacqueline —
fellow writer —
in admiration & with
gratitude for your friendship —
Kim
5/10/15

Poetry Mutual Press

WASHINGTON . DC

Fortune's Favor: Scott In Antarctica

Library of Congress Cataloging-in-Publication Data
Roberts, Kim
Fortune's Favor: Scott In Antarctica /poems/by Kim Roberts. — First edition.
56 pages cm

On the cover and interior: Archival photographs from the Terra Nova exhibition by Herbert G. Ponting, c. 1911. Library of Congress. In Public Domain.

Published by Poetry Mutual Press
3323 14th Street NE
Washington, DC 20017
www.poetrymutual.org

First Edition

ISBN 978-1-329-00621-8

Table of Contents

Prologue

In what has come to be known as the Heroic Age of Antarctic Exploration, 17 major expeditions were launched from ten countries. The secondary goal for most of these trips was to map the continent and gather data and specimens across a wide range of scientific disciplines. The primary goal was to become the first country to reach the geographic and magnetic south poles.

The Heroic Age lasted from the end of the 19th century through World War I, covering the years 1897 to 1922. Explorers of that time made their journeys before the advent of modern transportation, communications, mechanical or digital technologies. It was a point of pride among these men to test their endurance, both physically and mentally. Those who took on the challenge were treated in their home countries as national celebrities.

A typical polar party at that time would expect to spend at least two years away, in order to take advantage of the short polar summers when sunlight was still available and temperatures more manageable. The average temperature during the summer is 20° F, although along the coast temperatures above freezing are not uncommon. During the six months of winter darkness, the average temperature is -30° F. Often, in years when the sea ice was particularly thick, rescue ships could not make landfall, and a third year on the continent became necessary.

Since a party of explorers heading to the South Pole from Ross Island (the region where most British expeditions started) would have to travel some 850 miles, traversing the steep Transantarctic Mountains, they could not possibly expect to carry enough supplies for the entire trip and back. This required the building of supply depots along the route in the first summer season. That first season was also spent building a winter shelter in preparation for the long dark months ahead. It was only in the second summer on Antarctica that a push to the Pole could be conducted.

Robert Falcon Scott led two Antarctic expeditions. The first, the Discovery Expedition, took place from 1901 to 1904. Scott and his men made the first ascent of the polar plateau, reaching a new Farthest South record of 82° 17'. This book traces the fate of his second expedition, the Terra Nova Expedition of 1910-1913, and is written in his voice.

I. NOVEMBER - DECEMBER 1910 (LATE SPRING AND SUMMER)

Stormy Seas

The seas continuously rise, continuously break
on weather bulwarks. And they scatter clouds
of heavy spray upon the backs of all
who venture into the waist of the ship.
From four o'clock last night the southwest wind
freshened with great rapidity, and soon
we sailed just under topsails, jib, and stay
alone. The sea stood up and soon we found
ourselves in heavy plunge. We hove to,
still taking water over the lee rail.
The sea rose up like mountains. It rushed forth
across the lee rail and the poop, a press
of green; the ship wallowed in green; a great
piece of the bulwark carried clean away.

Ice

We've pack ice further north than we expected.
The floes, unlike the ship, prefer to rub
their shoulders. We are stuck. Or else the ice
will open out a lane mere meters' length
with the usual awe-struck absence of excuse.
Throughout the winter, ice sheets move and twist,
they tear apart and press up into ridges;
the bergs charge through these sheets, raising hummocks.
With summer, the sheet decays at the northern edge,
and heavy ocean swells can penetrate
breaking it into smaller floes. At night,
the sky turns burnished copper, salmon pink.
The bergs and pack reflect a palish green
with purple shadows dropped beneath the ice.

Fortune

The spirit of our enterprise is bright.
If there is work to do—shortening sail,
digging ice from floes for fresh water,
or heaving up the sounding line—then all
without distinction turn to it with cheer.
The men share a desire to sacrifice
personal consideration for
the expedition's ultimate success.
I know that Fortune's favor must be ours.
Fortune would be in a hard mood indeed
to let this combination gathered here—
experience, ability, good will,
enthusiasm, knowledge—such as ours—
to come so far and to achieve nothing.

II. January 1911 (Summer)

Loading Ship's Stores on the Dog Sleds

The fatuous conduct of the Adélies
delays unloading of the ship for hours.
The penguins leap upon our floe and waddle
toward us with grim curiosity
and a pig-headed, foul disregard
for their own safety. Howling strings of dogs
rush far as lead and harness will allow.
The penguins are not daunted in the least.
Their ruffs go up, they lean into the game,
the final, fatal, forward steps are taken,
a spring, a squawk, a red patch in the snow,
the horrid red. The incident is closed.
Nothing seems to stop these silly birds.
Then skua gulls reap gruesome satisfaction.

Winter Camp

Our hut should prove exceptionally dry and warm
with insulation (packed between matchboards)
of dried seaweed, sewn in quilted sacks.
Bowers built a bulkhead of case-wood
which shuts the officers' space off from the mens',
to the certain satisfaction of them both.
Meares is enamored of the gramophone:
we have a splendid record library.
The pianola's being moved in sections,
but I'm not sure it will be worth the trouble.
A first-rate building in a sheltered spot,
and towering above, Mt. Erebus,
elegant with its summit-flag of smoke,
unrivaled and sublime, for scenery.

III. JANUARY - FEBRUARY 1911 (SUMMER)

A Typical Pony March

The rugs come off the animals; nosebags
are filled for the next halt. One by one
ponies are taken off the picket rope
and yoked to sledges. Teams that get done first
fret with fingers numbing on bridles,
the nervous creatures straining at their traces
striving to turn their heads away from wind.
Yet still we wait: the picket lines are gathered,
several pony-putties need adjustment.
At last we're ready. Bowers takes the lead.
Finnesko gives poor foothold on sastrugi
and for some minutes drivers slip about,
but movement warms, and soon the column settles
into hours of fruitful, steady march.

A Good Leg Up for Next Year

The One Ton depot cairn is six feet high,
so large it should show up for many miles.
We tied up empty tea tins to the runners
of sledges planted upright in the snow
to act as light reflectors. We have cached:
seven weeks' provision bags of food,
plus eight weeks' tea, and six weeks' extra butter,
dog biscuits, sacks of oats, four bales of fodder,
a tin of cocoa, extra tins of matches,
and eight-and-one-half gallons of pure oil.
There's extra gear too: skeins and harnesses.
Two thousand and one hundred eighty pounds,
weighed tenderly, all measured. Latitude
of 79 degrees, 29 feet.

The Rival

Campbell sends a letter. Startling news
before which every incident must pale:
that in the Bay of Whales, Roald Amundsen
establishes an unexpected camp
along the Ross Ice Shelf. The proper course,
the wiser course for us, is to proceed
exactly as before. To do our best
to honor country without fear or panic.
I'll not speak of Norwegian treachery.
But there's no doubt that Amundsen's new plan
is a very serious menace to our own.
I guess he means to travel south with dogs
and forge a new uncharted route. And think:
he's nearer to the Pole by sixty miles.

IV. April - June 1911 (Winter)

The Home Station

After savage life in tents, the precincts
of our winter hut feel like a palace,
the light resplendent, all the luxuries—
to eat in civilized fashion, to enjoy
the first bath in three months, and have clean clothes—
such fleeting hours are treasured memories
to every Polar traveler (until
mere custom banishes the sheer delight).
While we were gone the scientific set
were making transformations. Sunny Jim's
meteorology corner all a-whirr,
parasitology at Atch's bench,
Nelson's and Day's biology cubicle,
and Ponting's well-appointed, plumbed dark room.

Routine

A settled regularity each day
is found: Clissold cooks and Hooper cleans,
Anton tends the ponies. Demetri
sees to the dogs. The men are steadily
employed with future sledging preparations
while officers do scientific work.
Some afternoons we play football on ice.
Our best athlete is Atkinson. Three nights
of every week lectures are given;
each man to speak in turn. So, for example,
Taylor on modern physiography,
Ponting on the culture of Japan.
I've asked each man to learn the basic math
for navigation by theodolite.

Midwinter Festival

In June, we had Midwinter Festival:
Union Jacks were hung about the table;
we sat to a flamboyant bill of fare
beginning on seal soup (by joint consent
the best decoction that our cook prepares),
then roast beef, Yorkshire pudding, Brussels sprouts,
concluding with some excellent mince pies.
Champagne in great supply. I made a speech.
As for our future, chance must play a part.
But no men better fitted could be found
and I thanked each in turn for giving me
their confidence. If happy fellowship
and good will count toward success, I say
that we deserve, surely, to succeed.

V. November 1911 - January 1912 (Late Spring and Summer)

The Barrier

We take November crossing our first stage,
the Barrier, with all our company:
the motor-sledges, ponies, dog teams, skis.
We set up cairns for sightings on the route.
Most men have goggles with a light green glass;
we find this color grateful to the eyes.
When sky and surface merge, it's dreadful work
to march into a pall of pure, dead white.
As ponies fail, we kill and butcher them—
we've taken to this horse-meat, and feed well.
Then, with the glacier gateway well in sight
we come on some exasperating storms.
How vexing to lie in wet sleeping bags,
feeling pitiful, when each hour counts.

Mounting the Beardmore Glacier

Here, numbers are reduced for the hard climb,
three teams of four, with each to haul a sledge.
We climb past talus heaps and huge ice-falls,
the surface slashed with crevasses. Our gear
gets fringed with crystals, beautiful but sharp.
Then when we reach the summit, I announce
the four more who'll return. They take it well,
such dear good fellows. We pitch in and build
a depot and reduce our load, then say
affecting farewells. I foresee our trek
will open with good promise; the terrain
is wildest desolation. Once we pass
the pressure ridges, all should open out
to windswept, open, undulating plains.

Christmas

We hauled all day and covered 15 miles;
ate so replete a meal it did us in.
Four courses: first, the pemmican, full whack,
with horse meat, sliced and thickened with biscuit,
flavored with curry powder. Next: sweet hoosh
of cocoa, arrowroot, and biscuit mash.
Third, plum pudding (I couldn't eat my share).
Then caramels and ginger for dessert.
After it was difficult to move.
We all slept splendidly in our warm tents.
This morning we were late to get our start,
slowed down by the effects of the plum pudding.
In general, the plain is flattening out,
our rise in elevation gradual.

Daily Marching

The marches are monotonous. One's thoughts
occasionally wander off to pleasant scenes
before necessity to keep the course
or surface hitches quickly bring them back.
On good days we get very steady plods
and swing together as a team. Last night,
150 miles from our goal,
I told three men that they'd be going back.
Teddy Evans took it like a man,
but poor Crean wept. And even Lashly looked
horribly affected. Birdie Bowers
now comes into our tent and we proceed
a five-man team tomorrow. Stores are good,
and all stows neatly on the smallest sledge.

VI. January 1912 (Summer)

Noble Companions

It's quite impossible to speak too well
of my companions. Wilson, our doctor,
is ever on the lookout to relieve
the small pains incidental to our work
and tough as steel in traces. P.O. Evans
designed our crampons and refit our sledge.
Details of manufacture and design
are his alone; he's indispensible.
Bowers seems oblivious to cold,
he keeps all records meteorological
and all provisions. Oates is a foot-slogger,
he does his share of camp work and withstands
the hardship well as any. I could not
survive without a single one of them.

A Black Flag

The worst has happened. Bowers' eagle eye
detected what he thought must be a cairn.
We marched on till we found a former camp:
sledge grooves, ski tracks, paw prints of many dogs,
a black flag. The whole story's here revealed.
Norwegians have forestalled us; they are first.
I'm sorriest for all my loyal fellows.
Tomorrow we must march on to the Pole
then hasten home with all our mustered speed.
All daydreams dissipate and I foresee
a wearisome return. The shock! Great God!
This is an awful place and hard enough
without reward of a priority.
We eat our hoosh tonight with black chagrin.

Ninety Degrees: The Pole Itself

Inside his tent, a note from Amundsen
with record of the five Norwegian men.
He asks if I will forward on his note
to King Haaken! I pack it in my book.
I figure out he beat us by a month.
We leave our note in turn. There is no doubt
our predecessors made sure of their mark.
We top a cairn with our poor slighted flag
and photograph ourselves: mighty cold work.
Then carry the Union Jack another mile
to leave it flying on a piece of stick.
Well, we have turned our back now on the goal
and face 800 miles of solid drag.
Farewell to our ambitions! Ah, farewell!

VII. January - February 1912 (Late Summer and Early Fall)

Troubles on the Plateau

Oates is feeling more fatigue, more cold.
Evans has bad frostbite on his nose
(the skin is hard and white) and on his hands
(his fingers badly blistered). It's high time
we cleared off this Plateau. The forenoon march
brought toothed sastrugi ranged in storm-tossed belts
that looked like a rough sea. We're low on food.
Now Wilson strains a tendon in his leg,
and Evans has dislodged two fingernails.
The surface is so changed since we passed out.
We came upon a field of crevasses
and had to steer more west. Our course must look
erratic, crazy. Weather skies appear.
We're not as far advanced as we had hoped.

Troubles Descending the Glacier

Plunging through our worst ice mess for hours,
at times it seemed impossible to find
a safe path through the turmoil. **T**urning right,
then doubling back and falling into chasms—
divided counsels on our course—the depot
doubtful in locality—my spirits
rudely shocked—our visibility
reduced by snowfall. Wilson finally saw
the flag of our lost depot up ahead,
with four days' food. **S**uch an immense relief!
We must repair the runners on our sledge.
We must get better starts, take fewer rests.
We can't let small delays accumulate.
We can't get distance if we don't have hours.

Petty Officer Evans

Evans can no longer pull the sledge.
He wandered far astern; when we turned back
we found him on his knees, his hands exposed,
his clothing disarranged. **A**sked what was wrong,
he slurred his speech and said that he had fainted.
He couldn't walk, a wild look in his eyes.
We got him to the tent with quick alarm;
by that time he was comatose. He died
just past midnight. Wilson thinks a fall
down a crevasse gave him brain injury.
Such tragedy to lose him in this way.
But calm reflection shows us this is best,
an end to our past weeks' anxieties.
A sick man puts us at a desperate pass.

VIII. February - March 1912 (Fall)

Scant Progress

The surface on the Barrier is bad,
no glide, like pulling over desert sand.
The absence of poor Edgar Evans helps
the commissariat, but in fit state
he might have helped us get up better speed.
Great difference now between the temperatures
of night and day—how swift the season comes.
We never won a march of eight mere miles
with greater industry. Now fuel runs low.
With every semblance of good cheer preserved,
we'll see the game through with the proper spirit.
But Oates' feet are wretched, bitten through
and swollen—he must be in agony
although he shows rare pluck and won't complain.

For God's Sake, Look After Our People

Should this be found, **I** want these facts made known.
The final thoughts of **O**ates were for his mother.
He said, "**I**'m just going outside and may be
some time." We have not seen him since. We knew
poor **O**ates was walking to his death; it was
the act of a brave **E**nglish gentleman.
We testify to his great sacrifice:
he bore in silence weeks of suffering.
We only hope to meet the end like him—
assuredly the end is close at hand.
Outside the tent, a scene of whirling drift
keeps us from starting. **B**y my reckoning
the next depot's a mere eleven miles.
It seems a pity, but **I** can't write more.

Epilogue

The remaining men of the Terra Nova Expedition had to endure a second long winter on the ice before they were able to search for and confirm what had happened to the five who'd gone to the South Pole. On November 12, 1912 a search party found the tent containing the frozen bodies of Scott, Bill Wilson, and Birdie Bowers. The search party, led by Edward Atkinson, retrieved Scott's diary, the men's last letters, and other personal effects. They then collapsed the tent over the bodies and erected a cairn on that spot, topped with a cross fashioned from a pair of skis. The party searched for the body of Titus Oates, but could find only his abandoned sleeping bag. The five men had died from a combination of starvation, dehydration, and extreme cold. It appears that Scott was the last of the five to die.

By the time the surviving expedition members returned to England in 1913, they were shocked to find their country gearing up for war. Most expedition members voluntarily enlisted in World War I.

In later years, two expedition members, Raymond Priestly and Frank Debenham, founded the Scott Polar Research Institute at the University of Cambridge. Herbert Ponting's still and moving photographs became an immediate sensation in Great Britain; sales of copies helped pay off the expedition's debts. The surviving members were honored on their return with polar medals and (for the military personnel) with promotions. A fund was raised to support the dependents of the five who died.

Over 30 monuments and memorials were erected to the five "tragic heroes" in Great Britain. Several Terra Nova Expedition members published books on their explorations. Scott's journals were first published in 1913 and have never been out of print since. I have modified his words to create this book.

Expedition Members

Officers

Captain Robert Falcon Scott, Royal Navy. Nickname: The Owner or The Skipper. This trip, later known as the Terra Nova Expedition, was Scott's second polar expedition; he also led the Discovery Expedition in 1901-04. His journals, from which this narrative is taken, were discovered eight months after his death with his frozen body, and published posthumously.

Lieutenant Edward Evans, Royal Navy. Second in command. Nickname: Teddy. Not to be confused with Petty Officer Edgar Evans. On the journey to the South Pole, Teddy Evans took charge of the motor-sledge party over the Barrier; when the motors broke down, he continued on, man-hauling a sledge. He was not selected for the final push to the pole, and turned back by Scott's command only 150 miles away. On the return trip, he became seriously ill with scurvy and had to be pulled on the sledge by his two companions, Crean and Lashley. Although he ordered them to leave him behind, the two men disobeyed, and he survived. He served in World Wars I and II, was promoted to Rear-Admiral, and was awarded a baronship, and named Lord Mountevans.

Lieutenant Henry R. Bowers, Royal Indian Marines. Nickname: Birdie. Bowers participated in an extremely harsh scientific winter journey to the Emperor penguin rookery. He was a surprising, last-minute addition to the final polar party. Because Scott had planned for four men, Bowers was the only one without skis, and had to squeeze into a tent designed for four. All food rations were also packed in units designed for four. But Scott depended upon his keen navigation skills. Bowers was short, at five feet four, with red hair and a large, beak-like nose. He was known for his toughness.

Captain Lawrence Oates, Inniskilling Dragoons. Nickname: Titus or The Soldier. Oates was selected for the expedition based on his experience with horses, and also his ability to make a substantial financial donation. On the final journey home from the South Pole, he may have been more predisposed to frostbite of the feet due to an old war wound sustained in the Boer War in 1901 (which made his left leg an inch shorter than his right when healed).

Surgeon Edward Atkinson, Royal Navy. Parasitologist. Nickname: Atch. Atkinson took over command of Cape Evans when the polar party left. When it was clear Scott and the others would not return, he had to maintain morale during a tense final winter on the ice before the ship returned for the survivors. He led the eight-man search party that recovered Scott's journals. In later life, he served and was wounded in World War I.

Lieutenant Victor Campbell, Royal Navy. First officer on the *Terra Nova*, Campbell was leader of the Northern Party, which wintered at Cape Adare, then, due to unforeseen problems with their ship, which got stuck in pack ice, they were forced to spend a second winter in an ice cave on Inexpressible Island under scant rations. Finally they hiked for five weeks to get back to Cape Evans, arriving just after news of Scott's death. Campbell later served in WWI, earning a Distinguished Service Order and the rank of Captain. He emigrated to Newfoundland.

Surgeon G. Murray Levick, Royal Navy. Levick was also part of the Northern Party that explored the Adélie penguin rookery at Cape Adare. Although not trained as a scientist, he was known for his keen powers of observation. He wrote a book, *Antarctic Penguins*, that noted the birds' sexual habits (which included sexual coercion, sex among consenting males, and sex with dead females). Levick later served in WWI and founded the British Schools Exploring Society.

Scientists

Edward Adrian Wilson, zoologist and chief of scientific staff. Nickname: Uncle Bill. Wilson took part in both of Scott's polar expeditions. In addition to his scientific knowledge, he was valued for his skill at drawing and painting. He led a Winter Journey, consisting of Bowers and Cherry-Garrard, to the Emperor penguin breeding grounds on Cape Crozier—a trip notable for taking place in almost total darkness, at extremely low temperatures. He then participated in Scott's final polar team. He was Scott's closest comrade; Scott's body was found with one arm around Wilson.

George C. Simpson, meteorologist. Nickname: Sunny Jim. Simpson set up one of the first weather stations on Antarctica, conducting balloon experiments to test the atmosphere, and recording temperature and wind observations. He served in both World Wars I and II, and was later appointed Director of the Meteorological Office in London. He was knighted in 1935.

Thomas Griffith Taylor, geologist. Nickname: Griff. Taylor was the first to map several sections of Antarctica. After the Terra Nova expedition, he returned to Australia, where he became the founding head of the Department of Geography at the University of Sydney.

Edward W. Nelson, biologist. Nickname: Marie. Nelson made tidal observations at Cape Evans, and took part in the sledging journey to carry food supplies to One Ton Depot. He later served in WWI, then became Scientific Superintendent of the Fisheries Board of Scotland.

Frank Debenham, geologist. Nickname: Deb. Along with Griff Taylor, Charles Wright and Petty Officer Taff Evans, Debenham explored and mapped the western mountains of Victoria Land. He was injured during a game of football during the first winter of the expedition, which very possibly saved his life, since it disqualified him from taking part in the final polar journey. He served in both World Wars, and worked as a Professor of Geography at Cambridge University. Debenham and Raymond Priestly co-founded the Scott Polar Research Institute, and Debenham served as its unpaid Director from 1920 to 1946.

Charles S. Wright, physicist. Nickname: Silas. A native of Canada, Wright did research in Antarctica on ice formations and ground radiation. He was part of the group that explored and mapped Victoria Land. Although he hoped to be selected for the polar party, he was in the first group of men sent back. He later served in both World Wars, and was knighted in 1946. He returned to Antarctica twice, in 1960 and 1965.

Raymond E. Priestley, geologist. Priestley was a member of the Nimrod Expedition under Sir Ernest Shackleton, prior to being selected for the Terra Nova Expedition. He was part of the Northern Party that camped at Cape Adare and Inexpressible Island. He served in WWI, attaining the rank of Major, and co-founded the Scott Polar Research Institute with Frank Debenham. He was president of the Royal Geographical Society, and knighted in 1949.

Herbert G. Ponting, photographer, cinematographer. Member, Royal Geographical Society. Nickname: Ponco. Ponting captured some of the best-known images of the Heroic Age of polar exploration, including the first known color stills and some of the earliest films made with a portable movie camera.

Cecil H. Meares, dog handler, Russian interpreter. Meares selected 34 dogs and 20 ponies in Siberia prior to the expedition, and recruited Gerof and Omelchenko as assistants. The three then transported the animals from Siberia to New Zealand via Japan. Meares later served in WWI. Although born in Ireland, he settled in Canada.

Bernard C. Day, electrician, motor engineer. Day was the motor expert on Schackleton's Nimrod Expedition prior to joining Scott's crew. Although English born, he settled in Australia.

Apsley Cherry-Garrard, assistant zoologist. Nickname: Cherry. Although rejected twice for the expedition, Cherry made a substantial financial contribution anyway, which finally persuaded Scott to include him. Cherry was one of the youngest men, had no real scientific background, and wore thick spectacles. Despite these obstacles, he was part of the winter journey to Cape Crozier, and the polar party as far as the top of the Beardmore Glacier. In later life he struggled with complex health problems and clinical depression. His neighbor, George Bernard Shaw, encouraged him to write about his experiences, and the resulting book, *The Worst Journey in the World*, published in 1922, is one of the best-written memoirs on polar exploration.

Sub-Lieutenant Tryggve Gran, Norwegian Royal Navy, ski expert. Gran instructed all of Scott's men in the use of skis. Born in Norway, he was recommended to Scott by another polar explorer, Fridtjof Nansen. He helped lay supply depots to One Ton Camp, and was part of the search party who found Scott's body. In a final gesture, he skied back to Cape Evans using Scott's skis, to symbolically complete his journey. He later became a pilot and served in WWI, but he collaborated with the Nazis during WWII, and served prison time for treason.

Men

William Lashley, Chief Stoker, Royal Navy. Lashley was a member of both of Scott's Antarctic expeditions. He was in Scott's last support party, turned back just 150 miles from the South Pole. On the 730-mile return journey to Cape Evans, he helped save Teddy Evans's life. He later served in WWI.

Thomas Clissold, cook, retired Royal Navy. Clissold helped haul provisions to One Ton Depot. While posing for Ponting on an iceberg, he took a bad fall and sustained a concussion, and lasted only one year with the expedition as a result. He later emigrated to New Zealand.

William Walter Archer, Chief Stoker, retired Royal Navy. After Clissold's injury and departure, Archer was made cook. He served in WWII then ran a catering business in London.

Petty Officer Edgar Evans. Nickname: Taff. Born in Wales, Evans was a member of both of Scott's Antarctic expeditions. He was one of the largest men, described as "beefy" and "bull-necked" and noted for his hard work. He was the only non-officer selected for Scott's final polar party, and the first to die on their ill-fated return. Evans suffered from bad frostbite, brought on by a cut to his hand that did not heal properly. He also sustained a serious concussion in a crevasse fall, and deteriorated mentally as well as physically, before his final collapse and death.

Petty Officer Robert Forde. Irish born. He helped lay out supply depots.

Petty Officer Thomas Crean. Crean, also Irish, was a member of three Antarctic expeditions: both of Scott's journeys, and later, on the Endurance Expedition under Shackleton. Large in stature, he was valued by Scott for his strength and experience. Crean was part of the party that laid supplies at One

Ton Depot, and was in the final support party to the Pole turned back by Scott. Uncharacteristically for him, when given the news that he was not chosen for the final push, he wept. However, this decision undoubtedly saved his life. On the return to Cape Evans, Crean in turn saved the life of his colleague, Teddy Evans, after he collapsed from the effects of scurvy. Thirty-five miles from help, Crean went on alone, walking for 18 hours straight, to form a rescue party. Crean survived both the Terra Nova Expedition and the subsequent Endurance Expedition, as well as service in WWI. On his retirement from the Navy, he and his wife opened a pub in County Kerry, which he named the South Pole Inn.

Petty Officer Thomas S. Williamson. He served on both of Scott's Antarctic expeditions.

Petty Officer Patrick Keohane. Irish born, Keohane was part of the first support party turned back by Scott on the polar journey. He was later part of the final search party that recovered the bodies of Scott, Bowers, and Wilson. Keohane later joined the Coast Guard and served in WWII.

Petty Officer George P. Abbott. Abbott was part of the Northern Party that over-wintered on Cape Adare and Inexpressible Island, along with Frank Browning and Harry Dickason (see below). He served in WWI, and died young from pneumonia.

Petty Officer, Second Class Frank V. Browning

Able Seaman Harry Dickason

Frederick John Hooper, steward, retired Royal Navy. Nickname: Percy. Hooper was part of the final search party team.

Anton Lukich Omelchenko, groom. Russian born, he worked as a jockey prior to the expedition, and served in the Red Army in WWI afterwards. He was killed by a lightning strike during peacetime.

Demetri Gerof, dog driver. Born in Siberia, he returned there after the Terra Nova Expedition, and worked as a miner.

An additional 32 men remained with the ship, the *Terra Nova*.

Kim Roberts is the editor of the journal *Beltway Poetry Quarterly* and the anthology *Full Moon on K Street: Poems About Washington, DC*. She has published poems in journals throughout the US, as well as in Israel, Canada, Ireland, France, Brazil, India and New Zealand. Roberts is a literary historian who has done extensive research on writers with ties to her home town of Washington, DC. She is the co-curator of the web exhibit *DC Writers' Homes*, and has developed a series of literary walking tours focused on such DC writers as Walt Whitman, Paul Laurence Dunbar, Henry Adams, Zora Neale Hurston, and Langston Hughes. Roberts is the recipient of grants from the National Endowment for the Humanities, the DC Commission on the Arts, and the Humanities Council of Washington. She has been a writer-in-residence at 14 artist colonies.

Fortune's Favor is her fourth book of poems.

Poetry Mutual Press is committed to presenting the very best writing available in modern poetry. We are committed to creating beautiful pieces of visual/verbal art that you can enjoy and treasure.

We are proud to present Kim Roberts's *Fortune's Favor: Scott in Antarctica* as a work that continues our growth as a home for vibrant modern poetry.

For more of our titles and to find out more about us, visit us at www.POETRYMUTUAL.org

Or write us at: POETRY MUTUAL PRESS
3323 14th St. NE
Washington, DC 20017
press@poetrymutual.org

Colophon

In designing this book we searched for typefaces that Robert Falcon Scott and his colleagues would have recognized. The text is in Adobe Jenson Pro with titles in Adobe Caslon Pro.

Adobe Jenson is based on the oldstyle type first cut by the Venetian engraver Nicolas Jenson in 1470. Considered one of the earliest roman typefaces, it enjoyed a revival in the 19th century through the work of English designer William Morris who praised it for its beauty and perfection.

Adobe Caslon is modeled after the work of 17th century English type designer William Caslon the elder. The earliest typeface of English origin, it helped to establish an English national typographical style.